FALSE
Summit

False
SUMMIT

John DesCamp

Wind Mountain Press
Portland, Oregon

False Summit
by John DesCamp

ISBN: 978-1-5323-3206-7

Cover photographs by John DesCamp.
Cover and interior design by Dennis Stovall.

Interior photographs © 2017 Jim Halliday.
All photographs used by permission of the artist.

Wind Mountain Press
PO Box 4448
Portland, OR 97208

For information regarding ordering, reprints, or
readings, contact www.johndescamp.com.

Printed in the United States of America.

Contents

Acknowledgments

Tacitus said, "Success has many fathers, but failure is an orphan." In the hope this book will be a success, and because it could not have come into being without several parents besides myself, two experienced and talented friends need to be recognized (or blamed, as the case may be) for what appears in these pages.

My editor, Dennis Stovall, continues to educate me on how to write with clarity and insight. He has been responsible for all the technical and organizational issues that surround the publication of this book. More importantly, his informed literary taste and dry sense of how best to express an idea have kept me from going off the cliff in all the ways one can when writing. Any rough spots in the poems are mine alone. He tried.

For the second time, Jim Halliday has taken on the task of providing images to accompany my words. His love of music, good food, and of the pleasure that runs through everyday life is evident in his work and amplifies the content in what I've written.

It's my good fortune that these two are good friends. Each has given me the gift of his technical skill and artistic excellence. This book wouldn't have come into being without them.

false summit | fôls 'səmət|

noun

In mountaineering, a false summit is a peak that appears to the climber to be the pinnacle of the mountain. But when it is reached, the climber sees it concealed the true summit, which is still in the distance. A false summit can have a damaging effect on a climber's psychological state by inducing feelings of dashed hopes and failure.

We shall not cease from exploration
And the end of all our exploring
Will be to arrive where we started
And know the place for the first time.

TS Eliot—*Little Gidding*

False Summit

From the bottom
The climb didn't look that hard
Sun warmed rocks and cool evergreens
Along the way.

A summit just seen from the trailhead
If you squinted and craned your neck.
Unseen: the steeper pitches,
The washed out trail and the deadfalls.

Farther along, you arrive at the place
You started for, only to find
It is not your destination
The summit is further yet
And even from this height
Can no longer be seen.

Eyes blinded by sweat and years
Muscles cramped, fingers numb
We yet conclude the joy is in the climb
And welcome each false summit

The real one will be our last.

Creation

Eternally, our mind replays
The drama of new consciousness;
The always changing now
Perpetually on the path
From was to will be.

But how did it all begin?
Nothing but waters on the earth.
In the midst of the waters, the one seer
And the seer's mind

Within the god, that first division came
Prefiguring all others
The watcher and the one who watches
Both in the god's mind but
Now two beings

With this first division, creation had begun

Valentine's Day? Really?

How did this all get started? The hearts, the candy, the flowers and, worst of all, the gooey rhymes about roses and violets.

The impulse to romantic love seems universal. And being human, once we have the impulse, we need to express it. Virtually every culture in the world has some sort of springtime festival of romantic love and the tradition goes back for centuries—back to grittier subjects like fertility and procreation. Predictably, the Islamic countries ban such things, but the ban itself suggests the tradition has long existed in their culture as well.

There are some edgy parts of the tradition. Not everyone has a valentine, or is necessarily happy about the one they have. St. Valentine was a Christian martyr, and the St. Valentine's Day Massacre occurred in Chicago (where else?) on (wait for it...) Valentine's Day.

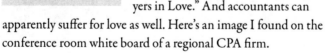

Peggy had many valentine cards while Viola only had one.

Peggy is a whore.

Competition and jealousy are more likely to rear their ugly heads on Valentine's than at any other time, except for the reading of a rich uncle's will.

The unlikeliest people (lawyers and accountants, for example) fall in love and have agonies of the heart, just like the rest of us. One of Jackson Brown's great tongue-in-cheek songs was "Lawyers in Love." And accountants can apparently suffer for love as well. Here's an image I found on the conference room white board of a regional CPA firm.

Not sure I want this person working on my tax return.

Well, if you have a Valentine, and I hope you do, be sure to do something caring and romantic for them, and not just on February 14th. We need to

be told, more than once a year, that we are loved. At least, I do.

Here's a poem I wrote it for those taking their first risky steps towards having a Valentine.

As It Is in Heaven

Caught in bare branches,
the full moon ceased its struggling
and watched.

Between past and future,
we ceased our struggling
and kissed.

With a relieved smile,
the moon rose free
and went about his business.

Valentine Secret

Quick guarded glances
Red silk in secret places
Inamorata

Vulnerability

Relationships are like seeds
Nothing grows
'Til the ground is broken

Being broken open is scary
Think how the earth feels
When the farmer
Starts about
His springtime business

Surprise Visitor

February snow
Green blur in bare birch branches
Winter hummingbird

March

What do we always think about when March comes around? I don't mean the rain; that's a given: the endless undulating succession of sunny days, thundershowers and soft rain that first raises and then washes away our hope for Spring. Not that. What I can't stop thinking about are the things that stuck to my Velcro mind when I was a kid.

First of course, there's the old vaudeville question "what day of the year is a command to go forward?" The answer, of course, is "March 4th." Da dum! I used to torment my sister Jean with this one. Her birthday was March 4th and since she was my little sister, she (mistakenly, I assured my mother) saw everything I said to her as some form of teasing. In retrospect, it probably was.

Then there's the old proverb. You know; the one that definitely smells like a stack of nineteenth century Farmers' Almanacs: "March comes in like a lion and goes out like a lamb". The Japanese (of course, you all know this) would say "sangatsu no raion (3月のライオン)," but I seldom say that myself. In fact, as a card-carrying Leo, I'm skeptical about this one because Leos are all about sun, brightness, warmth, light, and all the other good things that the month of March notably lacks.

Other months have a better time of it. For example, unlike March, the month of April can lay claim to a complex and edgy literary ancestry: TS Eliot's "The Wasteland" opens with "April is the cruelest month..." Now, that's a role a month can really sink its teeth into! But, more about that next month.

So, there you have it. March in a nutshell: a bad joke, a hoary proverb, and weather you would only wish on the US Congress.

And yet: March bears within it the beginning of Spring, and all the joy we feel at the birth of new leaves that erupt overnight from hard little green buds. No other month is so full of new life and beauty, moving in a punctuated dance from potential to actuality. No other month reminds us, almost simultaneously, of the gloom of Winter and the promise of Summer.

I wrote this poem one day when I was watching the sun and rain fall simultaneously on the West Hills and trying to assess how wet I'd get if I hiked to the Pittock Mansion. As it turned out, it was sunny and warm the whole way.

It often is.

A Song for Her Absence

Absent
But still with us
Lost to heaven
Where peaceful entry must be earned
Harvested early
But alive in our memory

She lived beyond herself
Beyond prediction
Love was her faith
Care and kindness were her prayers
A girl for a moment
Never forgotten.

To live in hearts of those we leave behind
Is not to die.

Tough Love

Whatever god there is
And I think there probably is
He or she is big
Big hands, big voice
Making the universe isn't a job
For midgets

Bigness is a problem
When you're trying to talk
To the little things you've created
And then, mostly, turned loose
To fend for themselves

When you do talk
Or reach into their lives
Your voice is deafening
Hard to hear what you're saying
And your big fingers squeeze them
A gentle correction can be fatal

All the same
If we're alive
After the conversation
I guess it means we've still got work to do

You're not ready for us yet

Ennui

Each story was so predictable:
First the flaming sunrise
Then the sapphire darkness
Shot through with iris light and evening stars.

And in each story there's a woman,
And lust and love, and loss. Each night,
Indifferent stars watch him
Stumble home from another all-nighter
Still drunk with need and desire.

A story, too often repeated, looses its meaning
The sharpness of metaphor fades
Leaves only allusions:
Short fat-fingered allusions
With rounded edges.

It's an absurd life sentence in
This endless twilight desert.
The dawn no longer rescues him.

The Cruelest Month

April, according to TS Eliot's opening lines from 'The Wasteland," is the cruelest month. Really? Maybe in England, but not here in Portland.

It's no wonder Eliot had bad feelings about April. The City of London lies at 51 degrees; the same longitude as Calgary. Contrast that with Portland, which sits at a balmy 45 degrees of longitude (equivalent to Genoa),

Those 6+ degrees make a world of difference. April in Portland brings a riot of sun, showers, and late blooming spring plants. Jolly old England is still mired in mud season and waiting for the lilacs to bloom.

And anyway, let's face it: where would you rather be for spring? Genoa or Calgary?

This isn't an oblique form of literary criticism; Eliot was working with the imagery he had available, which is what all poets do. But I wonder what he would have written about spring if he lived in Honolulu. Probably nothing. There are no seasons there.

I don't think anyone could write edgy verses about the weather in a tropical climate. In fact, I can't really think of any powerful seasonal poetry that has come out of a tropical climate. Everything is just too coconut/grass skirt cute to bear up under a complex and powerful climate image.

Anyway, back to the weather in Portland. For me, the arrival of spring is my favorite time of year. March gets our hopes up, as the neighborhoods explode with blooms. By April we've had a few warm sunny days, the grass is unbearably green, and we're intoxicated with the promise of more to come.

The dramatic changes of our seasons have been a driving force in the religious imagery of all cultures, and are no less powerful in Christian cultures than in any other. In every religion, the cycle of prayers and religious holidays runs parallel to the seasons.

Some of the most complicated and powerful spiritual imagery is rooted in nature. And maybe no religious imagery is more powerful than that of Easter. The essence of the season of spring is expressed in the image of Easter and the idea of resurrection.

This imagery of resurrection can extend to expressing the essence of all new beginnings and startings over, including the romantic kind.

Here's something I wrote while walking down the street, thinking about it all and enveloped by a warm snowstorm of cherry blossoms. And yes, there was a girl involved.

Passion Play

Good Friday

Cherry petals drifted past, unnoticed,
floated silently on swirls
of warm night Easter air,
stirred by passing cars and late night walkers
while we kissed; only half-aware,
and open—for a moment—
to each other.

With careful hands,
You laid your flowers down and waved goodbye;
taking yourself, the moment,
the soft feel of your lips on mine;
all of them gone with you.

Easter Sunday

Cherry petals drifting past, unnoticed,
lift silently on swirls
of late-day Easter air,
stirred by passing cars and Sunday walkers
while I stand, half-aware
trying to recall—for one clear moment—
your stunned warmth.

With careful shovel
I open up the earth, for just a moment,
carefully planting your blue-eyed gift;
and some part of you is resurrected
and returns.

Looking Back

Marsha loved me one time
In time, on time
And Karen trusted no one
But Marly was my music

Tension

Spring. Flowers burst from frigid dirt
Push upwards. The first spiders
Rig their corded webs
To catch the first insects

Across the street a 30-story tower
Pushes up from thawing ground
Dwarfing, and shamed, by the daffodils
In its concrete shadow

Spiders in hard hats
Weave their webs of steel and cables
Which are covered, floor on floor
By gray concrete

Cables tighten
Unseen tons of pressure
Hold the structure stable
Without this stress
The building can't withstand
The storms that come to shake it
From time to unpredictable time

Love's unceasing tension
Holds lovers together
When it grows too great
They cry out
But when it is absent
Love collapses

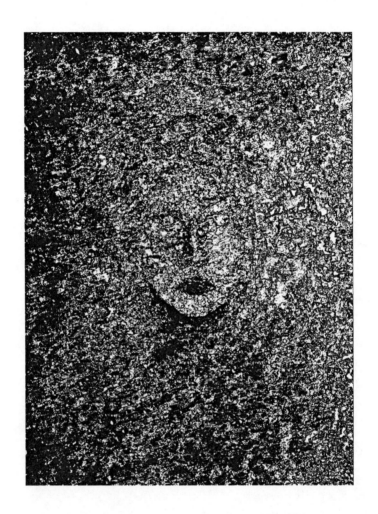

The Persistence of Memory

Each departing
More of her remains
Some days now
He can almost see her wise ghost
Watching when he wakes

Her bright voice hovers
Just out of hearing
But there
there, hiding beneath
The busy nothing
That crowds his hearing

Longer hairs
Have taken up their residence
In his brush, their color echoing
Her dappled skin

From a photograph her eyes watch
knowing, warm, impatient
wary, sometimes trusting
Her eyes speak silently, always
And he closes his eyes, remembering

The Myth of Sisyphus

The stories we have told, down through our time on the earth, are the record of what it is to be human. The characters and plots of our stories are, always, drawn from life. We tell stories to discover who we have been, who we are, and who we might be. We invoke the past in our attempt to make sense of our present and future lives and the lives of those others who are on this journey with us.

What we call myths, no matter what culture they come from, are just stories. Stories about how we got here, stories about why we're here, stories about what, now that we're here, we're supposed to do about the world and our place in it. They are stories drawn from, and deeply rooted in, the psychological truth of our human nature.

The Greeks were the greatest story tellers in western civilization. Their myths offer powerful insights into the nature of mankind—insights that are just as relevant today as they were three thousand years ago. Socrates, Plato and Aristotle used the myths as examples in their philosophies. Aeschylus, Sophocles and Eurypides created dramas which were both based on these myths, and which themselves became the central myths of later Greece. Along the way, Homer incorporated the myths in his telling of the Illiad and the Odyssey.

Somehow, the Greeks had a genius for getting to the root of the human condition. There's not a Greek myth that doesn't spring from a profound insight about human nature.

Whether the myths are about gods or heroes, their characters and their motivation are psychologically true in the unfolding of the action. These stories, more than three thousand years old, still shock and confound us with their sophisticated insights.

Since I first read it, I've been drawn to the story of Sisyphus. As Camus tells his version of the story, Sisyphus was a crafty and dangerous robber baron. He was also the wisest of all mortals.

He stole the secret of fire and gave it to humans.

For this theft of the gods' power, Sisyphus was consigned to Hades. There, he was condemned to ceaselessly roll a rock to the top of a mountain, from which the stone would fall back again by its own weight. The gods understood there is no more dreadful punishment than futile and hopeless labor.

Sisyphus pleaded to be released from his labor for a last visit with his wife. His plea was granted.

But when he saw again the face of the world, the water and sun, the warm stones and the sea, he refused to return. Finally, a decree of the gods brought him back. His rock was waiting for him.

Camus wrote his essay about Sisyphus in 1955. The Second World War had just ended. Europe was a devastated and hopeless place. Many of those who survived the terror and destruction of the two world wars had concluded the idea of a benevolent god, or of any god at all, was insupportable.

The Existentialist movement came to full flower at this time. The Existentialists saw human life as absurd. Absurd because, it was argued, if you conclude there is no god in the universe, and no afterlife, then life has no meaning.

They offered an alternative theology; one in which the meaning of our lives comes solely from the courage, wisdom and grace with which we live them. They argued for mankind's meaning to be found solely in our existence in the present and not from piling up good deeds prospectively for a later reward.

For Camus, one of the great Existential writers, Sisyphus was the absurd hero; the man who, in the face of the conclusion that there is no god, and therefore no ultimate meaning to life, chooses to act on the belief that life does have meaning; that life must be lived passionately simply because we have been given the opportunity of being alive.

When I first read Camus' view on this question, Sisyphus and his rock were just an isolated story line; another tale of the frequent conflict between gods and men, with the ultimate outcome always the same: the gods win. Rebellion against the gods, of whatever religion or time, inevitably leads to punishment.

Over the years I re-read the story of Sisyphus, but never thought about its deep consistency with the rest of the Greek myths. And I didn't see it as bringing any particular meaning to my life. It stood alone; another example of human pride and godly punishment.

Each of us has our story. Each of us is given a singular life to live out. And each of us is confronted by the singular joys and sorrows of this life. Setting aside the question of one's religious convictions, I believe the meaning of our lives lies only in the courage and grace with which we live them.

We each have our rock. The gods have fashioned an infinite variety: Failed relationships, distant children, financial struggles, disease, alcohol, rejection, toxic families, physical infirmities, the feeling of isolation. There are as many rocks as there are humans.

Our rock gives our life its true significance. Without our rock, nothing is demanded. Nothing is required. It's fine that we employ the gifts we are born with to carve out worldly success. That's the easy part; we're doing the things we love and have the ability to do.

But when we take up our rock, day after day, and push it up our mountain, knowing it will roll back down—knowing our success, if we do succeed, is fleeting—knowing there is no final victory except the victory of courageous persistence—when we call out every ounce of the best in ourselves in both acceptance of and rebellion against the rock we've been given—then we give our lives their highest meaning. We justify the privilege of being alive.

The myth of Sisyphus is simply this: each of us is Sisyphus.

We Die in Earnest

Late May; just another Spring
Flowers bloom, leaves unfurl
No surprises-its all happened before
And yet—
I'm grateful for the consistency
it's desirable at my age

If I were God—good thing I'm not—
I fear I might grow bored and
tired of the earth's recurring scene
set fire to the air, freeze the waters
curious to see what died and what survived

The Greeks were right to be afraid
of Zeus and his immortal line
gods without with patience or compassion
Who toyed with men for divine amusement
Agamemnon, loved by Hera
sailed the wine dark sea to Priam's Troy
brought heroes there to die for godly sport

Bion, a Greek poet and no fool
was wise enough to fear the godly spite
and cloaked his truth
portrayed the gods as children bored and cruel
"Boys" he said "throw stones at frogs in sport
but frogs die not in sport, they die in earnest."

Riverwalk

Gray river shivered
Gravid clouds fled overhead
May rain. The West wind.

The Sixth Sense

Our five senses: Sight. Touch. Hearing. Taste. Smell.
From birth, the five senses help us decode our physical world.
They help us navigate this place in which we find ourselves.
Individually, the five senses bring us the information we need.
They trigger emotions that range from delight to disgust. They
keep us safe, out of harm's way.

Think of the beach in August—the sight of waves lazily rolling
in and the flaming undersides of piled up cumulus clouds as the
sun sets beneath them; the invisible touch of the wind and the
cool wet sand on our feet as we walk along; the low background
hiss of the waves, the grumble of the undertow and the awkward
angular pitch of the gulls' cries; the taste of salt and iodine in our
mouths, just below our level of conscious perception; the smell of
a beach fire as the smoke drifts out from the dunes behind us.

When all our senses are engaged at once, the effect is over-
whelming.

Some argue for a sixth sense: a sense of balance. I suppose
that's an idea worth considering, but not in the way we usually
think of the term "balance".

I'd argue for a sense of balance seen as "knowledge of the
world". Not the knowledge that our five other senses provide
us, but knowledge of the world as a place with which we have a
contradictory and fraught relationship. Knowledge of the world
as a living organism; as a deeply written, unfolding story which
we must navigate.

What if we consider "balance" not in the physical sense, but in
the emotional and spiritual sense? This balance can only come
from our experience of, and our reaction to, the joys, sufferings,
successes and failures of our lifetime.

If balance—through knowledge of the world—is, indeed, our
sixth sense, then it certainly isn't something we are born with.

And, unlike the other senses, it isn't just a one-way process of gathering information from the world.

Rather, it's a circular, regenerative process in which we understand more fully each successive round of new information as we gather it and use this accretion of information we've gathered to navigate through our lives.

Knowledge of the world is something we don't have until we are middle-aged. It can't be taught to younger people, because it is learned only by experience. It isn't logical and it doesn't obey laws that are constant. It has no rules. Above all, it is not for free. It comes only from the unspeakably expensive tuition we cannot avoid paying as our lives unfold.

A friend of mine used to say "Experience is a hard teacher, and he is a fool who will learn by no other". I like the pithiness of the expression, but I think it's dead wrong.

We can't gain knowledge of the world through some antiseptic, hands-off, classroom process. We only gain it from the pain of our mistakes and our struggles over the years. We have to get our hands dirty and our knees scraped. There is no other teacher.

In the years that bring us to middle life, a sense of balance may finally develop.

When we notice that so much of our lives is, suddenly, in the rear view mirror; when we have begun to hate our used bodies, and the narrowing road north to whatever our future holds, we may suddenly find this strange balance. We find we can go on living—not by principle, and certainly not by deduction; not by knowledge of good and evil, but simply by a peculiar and shifting sense of balance that consists in making a daily decision to continue living with as much honor as we can. Like Sisyphus, we continue to push our rock up the mountain.

Discovery of this sixth sense, by which we navigate a world filled with war, compromise, love, and hypocrisy—isn't a matter for triumph. But there is heroism here; the heroism of duty and persistence. We no longer live by seeking the truth—if ever that was our goal—and whether there is any truth to be found.

Like Sisyphus with his rock, we simply accept the reality of our life and carry on in the world. We may not have, and cannot find, a reason for going forward, but we conclude that we can and we must do this.

But with this sixth sense, there is great risk. In the numb comfort of the balance we've achieved, we risk forgetting there was ever a time when we were young bodies flaming with new life, all five of our senses overwhelming us with the beauty and the heartbreak of the world.

We risk forgetting the time when we stood naked before the world, passionately confronting life as a serious problem—a time when we burned to find out whether there was a God—or not. A time when we wondered with all our souls what the world is, what love is, and what we are, ourselves.

It is mortally dangerous for us to forget the past as we face our future.

But the intensity of our early questions can fade as we become accustomed to the sixth sense; as we are able, without difficulty, to balance between believing in God and breaking all the commandments.

The sixth sense can smother all the other senses, leaving us balanced on a nondescript rock in a dull grey desert under a dead sky. And the sixth sense can blind us to the accommodations we've made, just when we most need to be a pitiless, detached observer of ourselves.

It can blind us to the outcrops of our selfishness, which are indecently exposed to everyone else—to our restlessness—to our inability to see the happiness in the world and to stop obsessing with our selves. It keeps us from seeing the fear behind our emotionally sterile arguments in favor of disengagement from the adventure of living.

Our balanced detachment can lead us to question whether there is such a thing as "Truth" and, if there is, whether it should be suppressed in the service of a greater need for compromise instead of clarity.

If we succumb to the sixth sense; if we fail to balance it with our other five senses; if we operate only by its gray dictates; if we cannot truly see any more, or feel, or hear—then nothing matters. The world we have played in, the bodies we've loved, the truths we've sought, the gods whom we've questioned: all are irrelevant. We become deaf and blind to them, safely and automatically balancing along towards our inevitable grave; drugged and protected by the sixth sense.

So here we stand; on the journey to our grey desert from our half-remembered Eden. But if our heart remembers—if we refuse to forget—we can still weep at sunsets and at the cold beauty of moonlight. We can still wonder at the waves of belief and hope and sadness that swell over us.

We can still be overcome by the beauty of the world and our human body; our hearts can ache or swell with a joy so great that oceans of sorrow can lie in the midst of it.

With appreciation for EB White, who got there first.

He Comes, Consenting

The Greeks knew the secret
They and others who traded human lives
For the favor of unyielding gods
The perfect sacrifice is one
To which the victim consents
Joins willingly in the offering of themselves

But more: the willing victim is itself
The perfect sacrifice. These others
The priests with obsidian knives
The king seeking fair winds
To sail for battle, are accessories
To the essential act

Led by a girl, a loose silk cord
Gracing his neck, the bull
Approaches the altar

He comes willingly
Knowing what others there
Can only hope: That in his death
He and the god are one

Vidi Aquam

I saw water
Coming forth from the canyon
Coming forth from the springs
Above the canyon, on the right side
Coming forth from the snows
That came before

And all for whom
The water came
Drank
And their thirst was refreshed

Give thanks for the snows
For the springs and for the water
And for what was before them
For the universe
That endures forever

Zen Christ

Feeling cosmically unloved?
Forget yourself
Don't believe your unbelief

Put on the yoke of necessity with relieved joy
Empty your pockets
Give everything to the wind
Then pay attention

The love never stops coming back

The Haiku

Haiku: three short lines
Syllables: five, seven, five
Condensed perfection.

Lathkill Valley Quartet

Written in the Lathkill Valley in Derbyshire, England,
whilst on a fishing excursion.

On the first day, as fishing was over and the afternoon
wound down, I sat in the garden of our stone cottage with a glass
of scotch in my hand, listening to the sounds of the place and
thinking how the pace of life is so greatly different for each of
the things we see around us.

These haiku began to arrive when the glass was about half
finished.

By the time the glass was empty, the rhythm of my life felt a
little more in sync with the things around me.

Good scotch will do that.

Afternoon at Rock Cottage

Midsummer's green light
Rabbits, pheasants, old stone wall
Pink roses climbing.

Remembering Venus

Along the Lathkill
Roses, campion, foxglove
Your sacred color.

Life spans

Mayflies hatch and die
New brown ducklings, chuckling coots
Patient old stone wall.

Evening at Rock Cottage

Green trees gone to black
Blue-black light inside the dark
Half moon setting west.

Ouroboros

Ouroboros is an ancient Greek symbol of a snake eating its own tail. It symbol-izes the cyclic nature of the universe: life out of death, endlessly repeated.

Down an ancient stone stairway
in the basement of the universe
He sits, bathed in the eternal light
and everlasting darkness of creation.

From His yellow cushion
He sees them all: the never ceasing round
of beginnings and endings;
the countless created things.

Observant, knowing, without emotion;
all good and evil, joy and sorrow,
lightness and dark, now and then,
contained in His circular self.

No need to choose or feel;
for all possible choices,
feelings, and states of being
are He, and He is them.

Worship Him:
for his clear-eyed, merciless wisdom.
Pity Him:
for He is not life, but only existence.

Summer Storm in Tanner Springs Park

The wind: warm, urgent
Erotically electric
Reminds him of you.

Of Dental Woes and Gratitude

A few days ago, I found myself sitting in my least favorite chair. You know the one; it's that 8-way plastic covered recliner that's upholstered in fake leather. The leather is the pale brown dried lima bean color of those lumpy shoes they sell to senior citizens at Wal-Mart. The chair has a spotlight pole and an attached tray for torture implements. The wet hissing sound that comes from somewhere behind your head on the left side completes the picture.

Remember that old Dustin Hoffman movie called "Marathon Man?" The one in which Lawrence Olivier strapped our hero into one of those chairs and tortured him with a dentist's drill? Ughhh! I don't remember a thing about the plot, but I'll never forget the horror of hearing the high whine of the drill and watching Dustin Hoffman writhe in pain.

Farther back in my history are dark memories, not yet suppressed, of a dentist my parents made us go to because he was a member of our church. The good doctor's fingers were permanently stained with nicotine and he didn't believe in Novocain (I think he'd gone to a mail-order dental school in North Dakota). Worse yet, he had an old-fashioned dental drill that was so slow you could feel each burr on the drill bit as it took a little more out of the crater he was drilling in your tooth.

I suspect this is the reason I quit going to church.

Fast forward to my recent trip to the tooth guy. I had a cracked filling and it needed to be replaced. Drilling was required, of course. It's always required once you walk through the door of your dentist's office. This fact is called *DesCamp's Law of the Worst Case Outcome.* This law also applies on any occasion I get stopped by a traffic gendarme. The chance that I'll get off with a warning, instead of a ticket, is statistically zero.

The dental assistant covered me with the *Shroud of Those Who*

Are About to Suffer and then fluffed around with long shiny sharp looking things. When she was finished preparing me for the sacrifice, there was the prick of the needle, the numbness that never comes quite quickly enough, and then a shrill scream. It took a second for me to realize the noise was coming from the drill and not from me.

As I lay there, cursing the entire dental profession, I realized there was an alternate reality; one in which I couldn't occupy that chair. With that thought, things began to look different.

There I was, getting my ancient teeth re-treaded for another 100,000 bites. The service was good, the place was clean, and with my health plan, it was almost free. I get annual maintenance and emergency treatment if I need it. And I'm in good hands with a professional who knows what he's doing.

Maybe it's just me, but I think most of us tend to notice the pain and inconvenience of things instead of seeing the benefit we get for our investment of time and discomfort. Dental procedures are high on that list.

I'm not saying go hug your dentist. It's always good to keep them at a safe distance. But I am grateful that my dentist and his dental minions are there to take care of me.

I'm not ready to start on an oatmeal diet just yet.

Mallards

Come on, Martha! This looks
Pretty much like the place
We stayed last year. This curb
This grass that's just across
The street from all the houses.

No, I can't find
The damned path through the bushes
To the little pond we nested by
Just keep on walking and
Ignore the cars. It's here
Somewhere

And no, I won't
Stop to ask directions
We didn't need directions
To fly three thousand miles
And we got here just fine

Besides, just listen to them
We don't speak their language;
And I left my phrase book
Somewhere in that marsh in Mexico

Love's Law

The life of love does not proceed
From church decree
That binds by words of eunuch priest
Who understands, perhaps the least
The paradox that wedding feast
And carnal joining of the beast
Lie mortally entwined within
The blessed act that some call sin

No civil judge or magistrate
Can legislate
The kindness and the lust we need
To keep alive love's fragile seed
As days move by and then recede
Co-mingled now with loving deeds
And we who love become entwined
In passion of a deeper kind

Your laughter lingers in my heart
When we're apart

A Trail of My Own

Sunday morning often finds me in the Columbia Gorge, climbing one of my favorite trails to a summit where I can see the mountains spread out in front of me. It's good exercise, and the peace and solitude are a great way to start the week.

Usually I get started at sunrise, because I like having the trail to myself. But a few months ago I got a late start on a climb up to Indian Point. As I drove into the Herman Creek Campground, I was resigned to sharing the Nick Eaton Ridge trail with all the others who would be out in this sunny morning.

But, what's this? The entrance road is partially blocked and a sign says "Road Closed."

There were no other cars around, but I decided to leave my car outside the park entrance and walk in to the trail head. Then my analytical nature switched on. WHY DOES IT SAY "CLOSED" WHEN IT'S ONLY PARTLY BLOCKED? I swung my trusty SUV around the barricade and drove up to the trail head. Here I found another hiker of like mind.

The campground was blocked off, but the parking at the trailhead was open. Good old Forest Service! They shut down the camping, which takes the time and attention of a ranger, but left the trail open for us "take only pictures, leave only footprints" people.

Up the trail I went. And in a four hour round trip, I didn't see a single person in my own private chunk of the wilderness. At the summit, I took a minute to thank the guardian of the place. Then I scuttled down the rock ridge at Indian Point to a precarious but spectacular perch with a view up and down the river.

Along the way back a light warm rain began falling and a haiku I'd been working on fell into place.

Dog Mountain Trail

Warm wind. August rain
Summer giving way to Fall
No going back now.

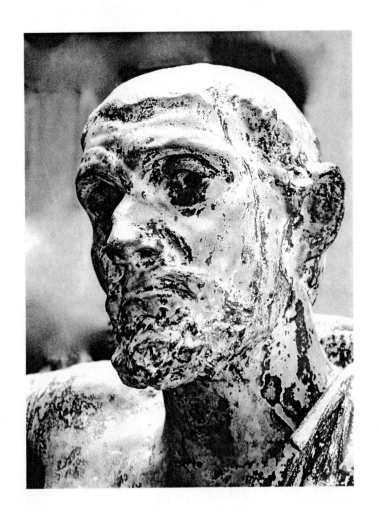

Sentinel

Bits falling off
These last two hundred years
I'm down to my core
But that's enough to keep me standing
Here above Hardy Creek

How long? I'm not good with numbers
But I was in my power
When Tatoosh the Thunderer
Shook the gods on Table Mountain
Cast their stones into Big River
Made the dam the Peoples called
Bridge of the Gods

Summers later, toothed steel
Cut down my children for men's lodges
My last sons taken, I still watch
A bent old man they left, unwanted

There's a grandson on the bank below
Next season he'll be taller than I,
Tall against the winds and snows
That fill the winter canyon

His seed will be strong
Strong to bring my family back
They will sink their roots in the stream's water
Below the steep hillside.

Each day I am diminished.
Time to let it go.

Waukeena Canyon

Bright susurations
Water over ancient stones
Waukeena Canyon

Solitude

All solitude
Is illusory, is inhabited
There's always an intruder
Hiding in the grass
At the edge of the clearing
In the place just beyond
The periphery
Of our vision.

Maybe it's us.

The Arrow

Being in love? At first
It's all about pain and risk

The good stuff comes, if ever
Further down the road
You always pay the tuition
Before you get the lesson

But take the chance
Stand out where Eros can see you
Maybe his arrow won't hurt that much

But the arrow has barbs, and can't be pulled
It comes out, in time, when the fever's gone
And you're deep friends or deeper foes

Endings are never neutral

Athena

I've caught glimpses of you
So often
In that slender wedge of time
Between desire and regret

Believed, on my long journey home
You would finally show yourself
That your peace would find me

It's been years of enchanted islands
And flawed goddesses
For each one, thinking I'd found you
I put myself on her altar
Handed her my knife and a match

And our joy was like swords
Pain and delight flowing together
indistinguishable

Is it you, this time?
Shall we talk?
There is always more to ask
More to tell.

One last time, Athena;
Love me as much as you can.

Aftermath

Three nights together
Three accidental nights
Three dark and perfect pearls.
Relief and yearning alternate
Now that she's gone.

Her absence, a quiet shadow
At the edge of his solitude
Unseen, but sharply felt
Like the silver sliver of frigid air
Slipping through his bedroom window
In the early hours.

Desire and apprehension rest
On each side of the bed,
Wait for morning to renew
Their argument.

Only time
Will untangle their dispute.

Traces

Tousled sheets
Like her hair
After the joyful reluctance
Of last morning lovemaking

Pillows crumpled
Hidden creases
Hold her scent and a shadow
Of her mascara

Yellow freesias
Lemon scent dying
Stand guard
Wait to see if she'll return

Her books hold the corner of his desk
Soft words soundless in the air
How can a place so full of her
Feel so empty?

Reverie

Sometimes
Near the end of a spent day,
He pushes back from his desk
Closes his eyes, imagines her

In a meeting talking, impatiently tapping
her leopard skin shoe
Hurrying through the airport
Talking brightly on the phone
As she sorts out the flock she advises
A fierce but kindly goddess

Other times—memories of
Their warm afterwards
Lying half-covered in the shaded morning light
Her hair a soft halo on the pillow as they
Warily dissected their lives,
Peered into the abstract, the possibility
Of what might be

After a minute
He opens his eyes, goes back to work,
But always with the feeling
She has been somewhere near him
if, again, only briefly

Sing or Be Silent

He fell in love with her sidelong smile
There was a future in it
equally rich in happy ever after
and heartbreak

No way to know how the song turns out
but to sing it through to the ending notes
That's always the question, isn't it
Start singing, or stand silent?

Paradox

We hide our imperfections
from ourselves and from each other
Knowing we all are broken
Desperate to be whole again
We seek love believing
only the perfect is loveable

Love will not flower in arid perfection
Only the rich dirt of knowing feeds it
Love knows all, loves all, forgives all.
What's left over, when it's all over
is all that matters.

So we have these choices
Give the gift of ourselves
broken, hurts half remembered
love because of our flaws
not in spite of them.

Or let life and time leak out
While we search for some Other
whose healing perfection
will make us whole

Who does not exist and
will never arrive.

The Argument

At first, certainty
Wise god in the center of my universe
I analyze, prescribe and dispose
Convinced of my conclusion, even though
I might not have understood
The problem

Then, a further thought
Conviction crumbles
Heart empty, thoughts blank, speech stopped
The sick feeling that, once again
I've misread the question
And this could be the final exam

Now numb with day and drink
What was and what might have been
Are equally true
And I must admit to all

West Wind

West wind at my back
Pushes me through small spring rain
Through the hopeful dark

Awakening smells
Damp brown leaf mold, early buds
Make me want to dance.

When the Going Gets Tough

I played football and ran track in high school. I wasn't really quick enough to be a great end, and I was too tall and heavy to be much of a runner, except in the 440. Those of you who ran that distance know that it wasn't as much about speed as it was about not quitting.

The head football coach was also our track coach. Mr Pearson had a large and magical supply of criticism. Most of it was pretty graphic, and it flowed freely when I missed a tackle or botched a play—events that happened too often. In the parlance of the late '50's it might have been regarded as "constructive criticism" in the sense he was telling me how to be better than I was. But it didn't feel constructive; it just made me feel worse.

One thing I remember, though: He loved to quote Knute Rockne, the legendary Notre Dame football coach: "When the going gets tough, the tough get going." Those words inspired me to become a credible high school runner in the 440. I ran it in under a minute, but just....

For some reason, Knute Rockne's words lodged themselves in an inner place. Over my lifetime, they've been a standard, not always achieved, for how to live my life. And I've felt my deepest admiration and respect for those who took up whatever challenge was in front of them and refused to put it down.

I believe Knute Rockne's words mean character is expressed in the present. It is immediate. Its essence lies not in what we have inside of us, but in what we are willing to bring out of ourselves and into the world; what we're willing to own about ourselves.

I want to tell you about a friend of mine who has given life to Knute Rockne's words.

Bill was a big guy: 6'4" and 220 lbs. In high school he was a gifted athlete: a T-formation fullback, and a basketball center with a soft but deft touch. He was fearless in the giant slalom and learned how to water ski barefoot a year before the rest of us.

If all that wasn't enough to make him seem like a teen age superman, he could play a wicked guitar.

Bill graduated from college, took a Masters in Accounting, and worked for a Big 8 firm for a few years. Then he got sick of the rat race and moved back to the small town we'd grown up in. He opened his own office. Within a few years, he had a busy and lucrative practice.

Along the way, he didn't give up the activities that made him who he was. He kept on skiing and he kept on water skiing. He stayed in good shape, and was so good on the fiddle and the guitar he was often invited to sit in with two of the local bands.

Life was good. And then, about 10 years ago, he was diagnosed with Parkinson's. The tremors, which at first you couldn't see, grew worse. His athletic life was over. Eventually he couldn't hold a pen, and he found it almost impossible to turn the pages of a tax return or to work at his keyboard.

Bill finally retired from accounting and sold his practice. But he was just too stubborn to give up on his life. So he bought a small tavern. Each day he sits at the corner of the bar, drinking water and talking with the friends who come in to see him. He never complains. He just keeps on with the bits of his life that are still available for him and he doesn't talk about what he's lost.

For some reason, Bill can still play the fiddle. For a few short numbers, the tremors stop. And he can still sing.

The principal role of the poets in classical times was to sing the stories of heroes: their deeds, their battles and, ultimately, their end. Bill was, and still is, a hero in my eyes, but the days of the Greek poets are long past, and there's no one to sing Bill's song.

I'm not going to sing for you, but I'd like you to read this poem I wrote about him....

Between the Bars

He can't sign his name anymore;
hands shake an up-tempo rhythm
like some damned digital drum kit
that you can't find the switch to turn it off.
So Peggy does it for him.

Still, he can pick up his fiddle,
squeeze the neck and draw the bow.
The tremors stop
and a high thin wire of golden sound
uncoils in the room,
grateful notes spilling like drops of sunset
as they slip to freedom
between the back beat bars
of his affliction.

Eyes closed, smiling that bad boy grin,
his renegade pulse is still
and time stops
for a few short numbers.
Then he opens his eyes,
hands the fiddle to Peggy,
and steps off the stage.

The silent beat returns
as she closes the fiddle case.

Iceberg

Nine tenths beneath the supple words
The poem lies,
Potent and formless, indistinctly seen
By reader or by writer

At the edge of knowing it looms
Thrusts up, shears the fragile self
In which we float
On our unconscious sea

Prayer for Compassion

Bow down before the wisdom
Whose only source
Is participation

Walk with those who suffer
Who have known the first words
And the endings

Be silent. Bend your knee
Before the highest wisdom
Which is compassion

And in the evening, laugh the laughter
That lingers in the half-light
Of our unanswered questions

Where Are You, Little Star?

It was past midnight. Garrett knew he'd be toast if his parents found he'd slipped out of the cabin. But that knowledge was a distant thing, like Venus rising over the water in the August sky: a fact, but one that had nothing to do with him. The temptation of a midnight adventure with Todd was more immediate.

In his gray sweatshirt and blue swimming trunks, Garrett sat on his family's overturned dinghy, facing the wide salt water expanse of Hood Canal. His father had dragged the dinghy up the beach in front of the Fielding's cabin; a back rest for some of the family and friends who joined their evening beach fire. Its keel had gouged a deep groove in the pea gravel. Rising moonlight slanted across the groove, creating a miniature canyon. Garrett imagined the dinghy as a monstrous turtle which had hauled itself out of the cool waters of the Canal and was laying its eggs in the still warm pebbles.

Across the Canal, above the eastern shore, Garrett could see the meager lights of Belfair and the faint glow of Bremerton. The moon appeared slowly above Bremerton's glow, and its trail stretched liquidly towards him on the water as it rose. A million stars shouted silently from the night sky. He could make out the Big Dipper and the Little Dipper above him to his left, and Orion to his right. But they were overwhelmed by the rest of the stars; so bright they, too, reflected on the night mirror of the water's salty surface.

A warm breeze blew off the water, disappeared, and blew hesitantly again, making the stars dance and the moon's path quiver on the dark surface. The breeze was pregnant with the smells of marine life, salt water, the muck of the tide flats and the green sweet smell of hay, cut that afternoon by some farmer across the water near Belfair.

About a hundred feet out in front of him, his family's speedboat was moored to one of the floats that followed the curve of the beach; far enough not to be grounded when the tide was out, but close enough that he could show off for Bitsy Henderson and her friends by swimming out to the boat, disdaining the dinghy as a crutch for parents and little kids.

Garrett had just turned fourteen. And he had just discovered Bitsy, whose family arrived that summer after buying the cabin next door to his parents' place.

The Hendersons were from Seattle. Fourteen-year-old Bitsy was a different being from the girls with whom Garrett attended junior high school in his small town. She used different slang words than he and his friends did, and had been to California and other places Garrett had only read about. She had a way of shaking her hair slowly and looking at him, her sapphire eyes peering intently through her bangs. At first, it seemed silly. Then one day he decided it was the most endearing thing he'd ever seen.

Bitsy's dark brown hair had a reddish cast. It curled loosely around her face and touched the tops of her sunburned shoulders. She was almost as tall as Garrett. Her slender arms and legs had a random dust of freckles and were covered with a haze of almost invisible tiny blonde hairs. Her seersucker Jantzen swim suit couldn't completely conceal the existence of her small breasts and a high rounded bottom, both of which were things Garrett couldn't remember noticing on a girl before.

Bitsy was the first girl he had really paid attention to. She had a profound female otherness, an essence utterly different from him and the boys who were his friends.

Garrett wasn't sure about Bitsy. When he was around her, he felt a nervous ache in his stomach; anxious that she like him but uncertain why, and slightly resentful that he cared. When she wasn't around, he thought about her and felt a strange sense of loss and grief, although at fourteen he wouldn't have called it that.

Half a lifetime later, he recognized this sense of loss as the essential feeling of falling in love. And he realized that, each time he fell in love, some part of him was sacrificed as he gave himself up to his latest lover. Taking this thought to its droll conclusion, his older self decided that if he fell in love often enough, his final death would be painless because there would be so little left to die.

But this was now, and Garrett's ache was mysterious and profound.

Idly, he picked up a handful of gravel and threw it out into the moon path. A quick chartreuse phosphorescence exploded around each of the pebbles. Garrett grinned; the water stars were back.

It was the summer of his fifth birthday when Garrett saw the water stars for the first time. One night, as he and his father sat in the dark on the beach, his father told him an Indian legend about some stars who left their tribe in the sky and journeyed down from the heavens to live in the waters of the Canal. They only showed themselves when called by their family in the heavens, and their appearance meant good fortune. Garrett loved the story, even after his seventh-grade biology teacher explained to the class about plankton and how these tiny sea creatures had chemicals which, at certain times of the year, made them glow in the dark.

In a reaction that foreshadowed his essential approach to life, Garrett appreciated the scientific information but liked the legend better.

Garrett threw another hand full of gravel and watched the pale fire flash again. He wiped the damp grains of sand from his hand on the front of his sweatshirt and looked over his right shoulder at the Walton's cabin, which was down the beach a few hundred feet from the Fielding's. The lights were out, but he was pretty sure Todd would still be awake in his corner bedroom, under the covers with a flashlight reading Mad magazine or one of his classic comic books. For a second, he considered tapping on Todd's window so he'd have a companion for the night.

But he wasn't quite ready for more of Todd's non-stop brand of manic craziness. Todd, with his horn-rim glasses and his lopsided grin, had been Garrett's friend for most of their lives. In the summer they frequently sneaked out at night to roam the little cabin community and see what people were doing after everyone had gone to bed.

Lately, though, Todd wore Garrett out with his constant jokes and flow of quotes from *Mad's* quirky cartoonists. Worse, Todd had been paying too much attention to Bitsy. Garrett didn't know why, but this irked him.

Yesterday he had deliberately taken a tight turn on one of their afternoon water ski runs. So tight that the tow line went slack and Todd sunk up to his waist in the water before the line tightened and he was jerked out of his ski, skipping across the water like a lanky rock.

Bitsy, who was riding shotgun in the boat, had squeezed his arm and giggled. Garrett's arm tingled and, for a few minutes, he had imagined he could still feel her light firm touch. A mean and delicious sense of satisfaction had swept over him.

> Twinkle, twinkle, little star
> How I wonder where you are.
> High above the clouds somewhere
> Send me down a love to share.

Across the cove, Garrett could hear music from the Kelly's place. Mike and Jerry, the Kelly boys, were almost out of high school, and were allowed to have parties. Garrett and Todd sometimes spied on them from the cedar bushes lining the boundary between the Kelly house and the driveway to the cabins. Last weekend he had watched Jerry Kelly lying in the dark next to Andie Paulson on Mrs. Kelly's favorite lawn chair. He was kissing her and their arms were wrapped around each other tightly. Garrett had felt a sharp and breathless wave of excitement as he thought about what it would feel like to have Andie's body lying so close to him.

For the third time, someone at the Kelly's was playing "Little Star" on the record player. This summer, the song was at the top of the charts on the Seattle radio stations. Big Al Cummings, the bearded disk jockey on KJR in Seattle, had called it the love song of the summer.

> Searched all over for a love
>   you're the one I'm thinkin' of.
> Whoah oh, oh, oh-uh-oh
>   Ratta ta a a a too-ooh-ooh

Garrett looked at the field of stars above him. The words of the song gave him a feeling of happy anxiety in his chest. He imagined himself on a stage, singing the song to Bitsy. No, he realized, that wasn't right. Yes, he was the singer, but he was singing to a star, asking it to send Bitsy to him. He knew his mother, who loved Bing Crosby and Frank Sinatra, would say the words were "silly," and the "oh-uh-oh" part was worse. But they captured exactly how he felt.

It was the first of countless times in his life when he found that simple, even banal lyrics, coupled with music, could express a feeling he was utterly unable to put into words. He looked up at the night sky for a star he could send his wish to.

Behind him, Garrett heard a door creak from the direction of the Walton's cabin. A few seconds later there was a whispering rustle of steps across the grass, and then a light, hesitant crunch as the steps continued onto the gravel and crushed shells of the beach. "Hey, Todd-o," he said quietly as he turned.

Ten feet away, Bitsy was walking towards him, stepping high

through the gravel of the beach like a delicate shore bird, her arms folded across her chest. Stunned, for a moment all he could think was that, in the angled moonlight, the impressions her bare feet left in the gravel looked like small craters on the moon.

Bitsy paused in the gravel at the end of the dinghy.

"H-hi," Garrett stuttered. He raised his right hand in a half ironic salute, then let it drop to the surface of the dinghy. He couldn't quite grasp that Bitsy was standing in front of him. The space he created for himself on his night adventures was highly private; he shared it with Todd only grudgingly when he needed Todd's encouragement on some of his riskier adventures. But most of the time he preferred being the unseen seer, wrapping himself in the night's black cape, watching the unsuspecting world from his invisible place in the dark.

Garrett felt a quick flash of resentment at Bitsy's intrusion into his solitude. It was mixed inseparably with the hot sweet apprehension that tightened his chest as he looked at her. She was dressed as she had been at the beach fire: a light blue hooded sweatshirt pulled over her blue and white seersucker bathing suit and her salt streaked hair, now black in the moonlight, tied back with a small blue ribbon.

Her bare slender brown legs looked different to Garrett in the moonlight. He wasn't sure why, but they seemed both strong and soft, and somehow vulnerable. They were completely unlike a boy's legs. He looked at them and thought he'd never really seen legs like Bitsy's before.

"Hi," she said, her voice quiet. "What are you doing out here?"

"Just hanging out," Garrett responded. He shifted his weight on the dinghy, but couldn't quite find a place to settle. He felt a sudden urge to tell her how much he liked being awake, alone in the dark, late at night, watching an unsuspecting world. Not knowing how to begin, or what she would think, he stifled it and looked at her, waiting.

"I couldn't sleep," Bitsy said. She brushed her hair back and pushed her hands into the pockets of her sweatshirt. "I think I got a sunburn today. I went out on the porch and saw you sitting here." She paused, tossed her head and looked at him through her bangs. Garrett's heart jumped. "Mom and Dad are both snoring." She paused for a second, and then looked at him again. "So, what are you doing?"

Garrett shrugged his shoulders. "Just hanging out," he said again. He felt light headed and slightly impatient, torn between the giddy delight of her presence and his resentment for the loss of his solitude. "My parents sleep like rocks." He hesitated, "and sometimes I get up and just look around to see what's going on."

"You mean, like, spy on people?" Bitsy asked. There was an excitement in her voice that softened the judgment in her words. Garrett was silent, gathering himself for an explanation.

Again she brushed back the sun bleached curls of her bangs. "Aren't you worried you'll get caught, or your parents will find you've sneaked out?" Bitsy's voice sounded as though she liked the idea, but was considering the ways it could get her in trouble.

Garrett shifted his feet in the gravel and his toes found the cooler stones under the surface. He leaned towards her. "I don't know," he started. He thought of one night last week. He'd climbed back in his bedroom window minutes before his father, on one of his nightly trips to the bathroom, had quietly opened Garrett's bedroom door to look in on him fondly. "I've had a couple of close calls." He thought for a second: "My mom caught me once, but I was already back and was sitting on the porch. I told her I couldn't sleep. So she just said I had to go back to bed."

Bitsy looked at him. "What do you see?" she asked. "Where do you go? Weren't you scared?" She shivered slightly. In the moonlight Garrett could see the blonde hairs standing out on her slender legs. Looking at Bitsy's legs made him feel slightly guilty, but he didn't know why.

He hesitated. Part of him wanted to answer her questions, and part of him wasn't so sure. He realized Bitsy would be impressed by his nocturnal adventures and he liked that idea. But at some level, barely perceived, he also knew he would be trading pieces of his secret life in exchange for her admiration. Something about that aspect of the transaction didn't feel good to him.

Bitsy shook her hair slightly, looked at him and pleaded: "Come on, Garrett. Tell me!" Garrett's chest tightened for a moment and a rising wave of possessive tenderness swept through him, breaking over the rock of his reticence. Why shouldn't he tell her?

"Well, I just sort of walk around. I look at the water. Sometimes there's a plankton bloom, like tonight, and its fun to stir up the water to watch the phosphorescence." He raised his right leg, bent his knee and put his foot on the bottom of the dinghy. Then he wrapped his arms around his folded leg and put his chin on his knee. He was startled by how quickly and vividly a memory came to him. "One night last summer, when my parents were down at the Alderbrook Inn with my aunt and uncle, Todd and I went waterskiing in the dark. There was this big trail of fire in the water behind the boat, and you could see where we were cutting back and forth across the wake."

Garrett stopped. Bitsy had a puzzled expression on her face and there was a little crease between her eyebrows. He wanted to reach out and touch her face.

"What do you mean, 'phosphorescence'?" she asked.

"You know. Glow in the dark. Like your little brother's secret Superman decoder ring." Garrett picked up a handful of gravel. "Look," he said, and flung the pebbles out over the dark water. Pale green stars blossomed on the water's surface among their reflected cousins from the sky, then faded and slowly disappeared.

"Oh, Garrett! What is that?" Bitsy asked softly. She moved forward a few steps and stood next to him, leaning towards the water. As she stared intently at the fading sparks, he felt the warmth of her leg, which was almost touching his. Then, in response to Bitsy's warmth, his leg was covered with the soft tingle of goose bumps.

"Uh," he said. He shifted on the dinghy and waved his hand vaguely at the surface of the water. "It's the plankton. Sometimes they have chemicals in them and they give off light if you disturb them."

"That's the most beautiful thing I've ever seen! How did you know about it?" Bitsy turned away from the water and regarded him. Her eyes were in shadow, but he could see she was looking at him intently. Suddenly, she sat down on the dingy. She was no closer than she usually sat when they were out in the boat, but somehow it felt different. Daytime's invisible barrier between them had dissolved.

"When I was a little kid, my dad took me for a walk on the beach one night and showed me." Garrett remembered the feeling of his father's big hand, the happiness at being out by himself with his father and the fun of throwing handfuls of gravel into the water. "There's..." He stopped, embarrassed and unsure whether he'd look silly if he told her the Indian legend.

"There's what?"

"Well, there's this old Indian story about some of the stars in the sky coming down to live under the water." He hesitated again. "I mean, it's just an old Indian story."

Bitsy turned towards him. Moonlight lit the right side of her face, leaving the left side mostly dark. She looked like a painting from one of his mother's art books. "How do you know about it?"

"Oh, from my dad. He has some old books about the Indians who lived around here, and I used them for a project in Boy Scouts." He was silent for a moment, looking at her. He felt as if they were the only two people in the world. Everything around them seemed muffled and indistinct.

Twinkle twinkle little star
How I wonder where you are.
Wish I may, wish I might
Make this wish come true tonight.

The music had started up again at the Kelly's. They looked at each other.

"Did you ever wish on a star?" Bitsy asked him. Garrett thought of his imagined singing performance a few minutes ago and felt his face grow warm.

"Oh, when I was little" he responded. "My mom says you should always make a wish when you see the first star come out." He looked at the overflowing sky, then back at Bitsy. "Looks like it's a little late for that," he joked. "How would you know which star to wish on?" Besides," he continued, "I don't know if wishes really come true."

Ignoring his joke, Bitsy answered "Does she say that thing about 'star light, star bright?' My mom always does. She says she made a wish every night when my dad was away in the war so he'd come home safe. And he did. So, I think wishes really work," she finished. She sounded a little put out with his skepticism.

Garrett slid down off the dinghy and sat on the gravel. He sat facing the water with his legs stretched out. After a moment, Bitsy followed him. As she slipped down, the gravel made a soft dry whispering crunch. Settled, they leaned back on the dinghy's side and looked out over the water. Like a song that fades in and out of hearing, tendrils of breeze made shivery patches on the moon's path. Bitsy sat so close their shoulders almost touched. He could feel her warmth along his right leg and the goose bumps were back.

"Well", she continued as the 'oo-oo-oo' ended, "I like that song." She paused again. "Don't you like it?" There was a teasing challenge in her voice. They looked out over the water and Garrett idly threw a single pebble into the dark mirror. A liquid star bloomed and began to fade, the ripples from the pebble undulating across the moon path.

"There," he said. "We can wish on that one." Garrett was conscious of a sudden shift in the energy between them. He felt a sweet sense of apprehensive joy, a delicious feeling of danger in his throat; he was wrapped in soft cotton again, Bitsy the sole focus of his attention.

She turned to look at him, her eyes reflecting the moon light, and took his right hand in her left one. Her hand felt strong, but it was warm and soft. He could feel the sticky dampness of salt water and a few tiny pieces of shell which had stuck to her palm when she braced herself on the gravel as she slid down next to him.

"OK," she replied, looking at him with a smile. "But you can't tell anyone your wish. If you do, it won't come true." Bitsy sounded grave as she said this, but Garrett had the feeling she was teasing him. "Anyway", she continued, with a practical tone, "you'd better throw another rock. The star's gone away."

Bitsy's warm grip tightened slightly on Garrett's right hand; a signal he interpreted as a warning he shouldn't let go. With his left hand he picked up another pebble, larger than its companions. He held it for a moment, then stretched out his palm to Bitsy. "Here", he said, "you throw it."

She took the pebble deliberately, holding it between her right thumb and forefinger. Letting it drop into her cupped palm, she tossed it overhand into the water in front of them as she said "make a wish."

No thought, no words came to Garrett, only a vivid picture: Bitsy's head tilted back as he kissed her. He imagined the light touch of her hair on his face, her closed eyes with lashes dark against her sparsely freckled cheeks and the warm stillness of her lips. He could feel the thumping engine of his heartbeat.

Without thought, Garrett leaned towards her and found her

welcoming face upturned towards his. He held his lips to hers, shifting awkwardly so he could avoid letting go of her hand. Bitsy sighed. Garrett opened his eyes, still kissing her and found her looking at him. There didn't seem to be anything to say. His heartbeat boomed in his ears as he straightened up.

They looked at each other and Bitsy gave him a faint grin. There were little crinkles in the corners of her eyes.—"I got my wish," she said softly.

Hood Canal September 30

A long time
Since I've been on these waters

It was summer
A million stars in the black sky
An antic breeze
The lights of Belfair in the distance
The smell of just-cut hay
Fireflies in the water
A freckled girl close
On the night beach.

Is that how it was? Did I say it right?
I'm not sure
The past is now another country
And I no longer speak the language

Dry Creek

Dry. Each day more barren
Dessicated grass and scorched sand
Along the banks, baked mud
And shattered boulders
Lizards skitter where trout darted

Black clouds and thunder. Rain
In the next valley
Nothing here but arid hope and
The growing certainty
Of a parched end

Will there be water? I pray
To the god who holds it—who
Withholds it. No answer.
Dry rain again today.

Borrowed Times

In this meager year
I've come to depend
On the kindness of friends

And friends will get you
Through times of no money
Better than money will get you
Through times of no friends

Post Breakup Writer's Block

No words
No combinations of words
No ideas—no thoughts at all
Then and when erased
Banished by the impact of now

Nothing in the tool kit
But platitudes, conclusions
Time-worn adjectives—like that one—
Hackneyed expressions, aphorisms
Things said that, on further thought
Need to be said differently
Or can't, really, be said at all

The dry dust of instant coffee
In the bottom of my cup
No scent, no aroma, no feeling, no life
No steam without the boiling water

Reykjavik—Eddies in the Stream

I'm walking down Skólavörðustígur in the northern half light of a late September day. It isn't a street name that would lead you to believe it was painted with rainbow stripes for its entire length. As with many Nordic words, this one is a compound of three different words, "skóli," "varða," and "stígur." Skóli means school, varða means cairn and stígur is a path. Colloquially, City Center Street. You'd be correct if you suspected it lead to the city's center. It does.

Two and three story masonry buildings line the street in conservative shades of gray, cream, and brown. Bright red and blue doors shout out from time to time. The blue-gray cloud cover is like a knit cap over the city. Light leaks out of the sky like a spent candle. Colors are muted. The sombre sky dilutes brightness of any kind.

Icelandic interiors are as subdued and monochromatic as the landscape. I suppose that's no surprise; it's the world around us that establishes our inner palette. As Camus observed, "A face that toils so close to stones is already stone itself."

The marine climate here is the same as everywhere else along the Atlantic; no salt in the air. Why doesn't the Atlantic have a rich, fetid, organic marine smell like the Pacific does?

Parks are many, but trees are few, and those few feel less like a natural occurrence or organic element than an artifact; a modern aesthetic imposition on the wild, flat rocky landscape

An old cemetery wears its cloak of evergreens, mixed among deciduous trees that are dying for the season. There's a gravestone for someone born in 1856.

The reflecting pond in front of City Hall is filled with white geese and mottled ducks and gulls.

Knit caps, mufflers, boots, parkas, and wool coats are the uniform of the day in a land of perpetual autumn. Stony fields and dead grasses stretch to the perfect volcanic cones, miniature Mt. Fujis, on the horizon.

Hallgrímskirkja is the national cathedral—its design composed of equal parts of Riems cathedral and a Viking helmet. The cathedral's deceptive mass looms over the city, a presence larger than its modest size. Inside, it's all spare surfaces and muted intense monochromatic light.

Along the walls, like hip, non-religious stations of the cross, abstract paintings echo but transgress the images from traditional religious art. An huge pipe organ fills the entire rear of the church with its ranks of notched silver pipes, and seems to have been intended for a much larger space. Japanese tourists walk the aisles quietly, bemused to find in this muted city a design that seems to be made up of Norse and Zen esthetic influences in equal measure.

Over the weekend, a cartoon Viking image was painted on the surface of the entire parking lot across from my hotel. It is now being washed to oblivion by a city employee in bright waterproofs and wellies. He wields a hissing steam pressure washer—a post-modern metaphor, maybe, for the gradual dilution and obliteration of the original Icelandic culture by recent waves of tourists and dreamers seeking the new best thing.

The tourists, and the cruise ships floating like awkward steel blimps on the surface of the harbor, make me think of Omar Khayyam:

"I wonder what it is the cruise ships bring,
One half so precious as the place they come."

For dinner, I visit a recommended restaurant that looks out over the rainbow street. Because I'm early, I manage to secure a window table so I can watch the street as people head home for the evening. Dense, elastic rye bread with salty butter and Hendricks gin are a good start to my meal. I'm offered a menu that lists conventional northern European fare, along with horse, whale, and puffin—a testimony to man's willingness to eat protein from any available source. And Herb Caen strikes again, here in far off Iceland: "mayonnaise" spelled "mayonnese."

As the sky darkens and the light in the restaurant grows brighter, I change roles with the people walking along the street, and slowly slip from being the observer to the observed.

Dogs don't seem to be common here, but maybe they're on the menu in some less tourist-oriented restaurant. I make my first dog sighting while eating dinner: a German Shepherd puppy dragging his mistress up the street with the leash in his teeth. The low thumping of quasi-original Iceland rock makes a backdrop for the clink of glasses and the sharp arrhythmic conversations behind me.

Iceland contemporary music seems prepackaged and derivative—too much Barry Manilow and not enough Janis Joplin. It has none of the edgy electrical energy that characterizes British and American rock. I suppose a culture of 300,000 people can't be anywhere near the sharp edge of a world phenomenon, Bjork notwithstanding. But, at its best, the music is a small and distinct clear stream that feeds one of the rivers that run to the eternal musical ocean.

I walk back to my hotel through narrow lanes that wind like eddy currents away from the main street. It's dark and there are few people on the side lanes. The warm lights of the hotel lobby beckon from the top of the cobblestone walk.

Hardy Ridge

First day of autumn
On the trail to Hardy Ridge
Dying leaves float down.

Equinox

Dry boards breathe new rain;
sharp smell of dust. Summer dies
giving birth to autumn.

August Haiku

Velvet summer night
A park bench after dinner
Only this moment.

For Alice

Somewhere, there's a photo of the whole thing
Mary and Alice, sitting in the cockpit of Stella Maris
tanned, skimpy bathing suits, beers in their hands
There were always beers somewhere on the boat
Even if the sandwiches had been left at the dock

Carl, smiling that bad boy grin,
Hauls on the main sheets while, out of sight in the stern,
I'm manning the tiller, praying I don't screw up
As we come around hard just upriver from Jarv's jetty
One last spinnaker reach before we come about
And head back to the club for more beers
And the Sunday party.

Alice is clutching some poems she wrote
In the mock-heroic style
("The Summer of the Vorst Platz" comes to mind)
Telling conflicting stories of her golden princess
And the dark prince she somehow married
The endings were uncertain, and
I lost track of them years ago

Some of the undercurrents weren't in the river
A few in plain sight, if we'd been able to see
But you had to be older than any of us were, and
Full partner, as none of us were, yet
To the relinquished dreams and deferred hopes
we'd each inherited from the prior generation.

I miss her; have missed that particular Alice
For more than 45 years. She's still out there, somewhere
Tipping back a drink, lighting a cigarette
Living a heedless, wild, in the moment Zen of a life
That never looked back.

Cycles

This year the Autumn Equinox takes place in the northern hemisphere on September 22nd.

From a left brain point of view, the equinox is an astronomical event in which the plane of Earth's equator passes through the center of the Sun, which occurs twice each year, around the 20th of March and the 23rd September.

On each of the two equinoxes, day and night are of approximately equal duration in each longitude of the planet.

From a right brain point of view, the equinoxes are a mysterious occurrence; a time when events in the outer world reflect or foreshadow the cycles of our lives. Autumn is the beginning of the end and the end of the beginning. Three quarters of the year are finished. Winter's dormancy, Spring's beginning and Summer's growing are in the rear view mirror.

Days and nights are cooler. The sun's light shifts from warm yellow to a cooler white. There's a scent of smoke in the air. For countless generations, this is the time when mankind has brought in the harvest, feasted generously, and begun preparing for the dying of the year and the waking hibernation of Winter.

Primitive religions of all the temperate zone cultures found a strong correspondence between the cycles of the year—dormancy followed by rebirth in Winter, planting in Spring time, tending crops through the Summer, and harvest in the Autumn—and the cycles of our lives:

- Birth and adolescence
- Growth and maturity
- Harvesting the seasoned wisdom of old age
- Death and the coming of a new generation

We can see this birth/growth/death cycle in the central areas of our lives: in our relationships, our careers, in the things we've chosen to build or create. Each reflects this yearly cycle of which the equinoxes and solstices are the mileposts.

Down through the centuries, the solar cycle has been intertwined with every culture's art, with its architecture, with its music, and most deeply in its religion. The central events of the Christian faith are a great example: Christ's birth, maturation, death, and resurrection.

For architecture, think of Stonehenge and the Egyptian and Aztec temples that were aligned to show the precise day of the equinoxes and the Summer and Winter solstices. For music, think of works as diverse from one another as the 1964 jazz standard by John Coltrane, the 1967 album by Sergio Mendes and Brazil '66 and the 1975 album by Styx.

Autumn weddings are for older lovers; for those whose planting and nurturing has been done elsewhere and now meet at the harvest for the first time.

I wrote this poem sitting on a ledge above the Columbia River. High thin clouds were scrawled across the pale sky. In the wind coming down the Gorge, maples and larches were losing their leaves in stuttering golden showers. The whistle of the train heading east had a reflective note it hadn't had in Spring, when it sounded excited to be on the road to a new adventure.

Let's just say I was more conscious than I sometimes am that the end is closer than the beginning.

Autumn on the River

Within each life, the little deaths
The slow tearing from ourselves
Of a world in which delight lies somewhere
Between boredom and confusion

Deaths of parents, family, pets
And others loved and unloved.
Strength and senses dim
Only habits grow fiercely stronger

Classmates depart. The old house
Is torn down for a new apartment
We struggle to keep what capacity we still hold
To love that which is other than ourselves

Seasons hurry off the stage
Stepping on each other's heels
In their unseemly haste
To be on their way
To the next best thing

Ahead, the river grumbles
Falls away in soundless mist
Voices from shore are faint
Those inside grow stronger

The pace of leaving quickens
As we round the last bend
No reason to hold back

With so much taken
There's so little left to lose

Theory of Relativity

"The measurement of time is relative to the observer."

Einstein, Planck
All of them since Maxwell
Knew time's relativity, knew
Celestial bodies, gravity and light
Invisible rays and dark matter

And all of them missed the point. This wasn't
Something new or unusual in the universe
Not a sudden discovery of science
Lovers discovered it too, eons ago
In a different laboratory

As long as we have loved,
Even physicists have known: that
Love is composed of invisible rays, that
Life is filled with light
And with dark matter, that
Our lover's body is celestial, with
Its own inexorable gravity

That when we are parted
Time is infinite, that
always, time together
Is infinitely short, that
always, the speed of leaving
Is the speed of light, that
Eternity passes
Before the return.

Past and future fill
The eternal present
The black hole that opens up
When you are gone

Autumn Rain

He leaves her. Leaves fall.
Small grief inside the great—her
tears in autumn rain.

Devils' Rest Trail

Wet, leaf-covered trail;
low skies. Indifferent tears
fall from Autumn clouds.

Pumpkin on tree branch;
Halloween on Devils Rest.
I'm here! Trick or treat?

Thanksgiving

It's hard to get into the habit of saying "thanks." The days go by and my frustrations and struggles can sometimes overshadow the realization that I've got a pretty good life. This Thanksgiving holiday is a reminder of my need to be thankful.

And yet—if you think about it, all the holidays are about giving thanks for something. There's Mother's Day and Father's day. There are all the religious holidays on which we give thanks for our relationship with our Creator and for all the good things that have come to us in our lives. There are all the civic holidays on which we give thanks for the founding of our country, and for the men and women who worked, fought and died for it.

The idea of a single day of thanksgiving misses the point. What about the other 364 days? Weren't there things to be thankful for on each one of them? Maybe the idea of Thanksgiving needs to be more than just a one-day event on our calendar—maybe it needs to be a permanent state of mind.

Sitting here on the shank end of a Monday (and it has been a truly repulsive Monday) I was chewing on some frustrations and disappointments that sprang up today like weeds in the garden of my Thanksgiving week.

To get out of this mood, I decided to reflect on the things for which I'm thankful, and started a list. About 14 items later, it was clear I needed to shut up and stop complaining.

Here are the top things on my list. Each one is something I can imagine my life without, but it would be a much different life. And I kind of like the one I've got. It isn't perfect, but its mine. Make your own list and, if you feel like it, share it with me.

- My children
- My grandchildren
- My brothers and sisters
- Deep friendships with very special friends

- Good health
- Interesting work
- Great clients
- Mentors who have helped me along the way
- Poetry, and my new book
- Living in Portland
- The Columbia Gorge
- All the books that have become my close friends
- Being in my 70's
- The surprising generosity of everyday life

Thanks! I'm grateful for you, too, because you are part of my world, and you read what I write. And that's a real gift to me. So, here's a Thanksgiving haiku for you.

> For what we're given
> From what we have been spared
> Daily gratitude

Thank you, and Happy Thanksgiving!

For Elizabeth

The deepest form of love is
patient observation.

Ten years old,
at the desk in my solitary room
building model airplanes,
the rough noise of the family
safely beyond my door.

You, the only one I'd let in,
my silent witness, even when I savaged you
as some part of the construction process
—pine struts, balsa wood, paper and, especially,
the hot heady smell
of glue and banana oil—
went badly.

Quiet but not passive
you left, along with your 5-year old dignity
when my displaced anger singed you
But you always returned.

The warmth of your regard
Is with me these years later;
as I turn out the light,
pull the cool sheets over me,
give thanks for what solitude brings,
and remember your patient love.

Belated Conversation

My parents' graves
Are at the top of a hill
I walk there sometimes
It's not too far
Hoping for the one conversation
We were never able to have.

We're closer now than we were
It's life that keeps us apart, not death
Like the audience at an absurd play
We don't really understand the characters
Until they've left the stage.

Their voices are faint
But clearer as the years pass
My hearing has improved
With age.

Aging and Insight

We've all received them: angry e-mails from a family member or an old friend, warning us of the treachery and stupidity of the left wing, the right wing, the Muslims, the Oregon Bicycle Alliance, the whatever. Last week I hit the jackpot: I got two of them in the same morning.

And to make it even better, there was one from each side of the political fringe. One of my friends is convinced the State of Texas requires the use, in all of its schools, of textbooks that teach the world is only 6,000 years old. My uncle, on the other hand, is 91. He shouldn't be allowed to drive a computer or visit the internet without adult supervision. And he believes 93% of all Hispanic people in the US are on welfare and are planning to take over California and make everyone speak Spanish.

This is all funny...sort of. It seems that as we age, many people are more and more angry with the world.

Personally or by observation, we all know the difficulties of aging:

- Physical decline
- Sickness
- The fear that our money will run out before we do
- The loss of those we love
- The boredom that can accompany retirement
- The task of finding new significance at the end of an active and productive life

As Bette Davis said, "old age is not for sissies."

But worst of all is the danger we often don't see: the closing of our minds, the hardening of our mental arteries, the loss of a flexible mind in the face of a new world that shows itself to us relentlessly, each day, in more puzzling, frustrating, and interesting ways.

There's a risk that, in our work of aging, we grow bitter—seeing ourselves as justifiably disappointed in a world that refuses to conform to our strident expectations of what it should give us, of how people should be. There is a temptation to declare it all worthless—to pick up our marbles and go home if people don't "play nice"—don't play by our rules.

For some reason, this dissatisfaction in later age seems more prevalent in men than in women. Maybe that's because society still offers meaningful roles for women as they age, even if many of these roles are largely pre-feminist. The role of grandmother, good friend, confidant, wise counselor, preparer of comfort meals, family historian...many women seem to move naturally into these roles as they age.

Men, on the other hand, seem to have a harder time. When you've been a warrior for 50 years, it's hard to put down your sword—hard to find significance in a role that requires listening instead of talking; that requires analysis instead of action; and, most of all, that requires us to accept that we must trade our power for patience if we're going to remain significant in the lives of others—if we're going to step up to the new role our family, our friends, and the world now need us to occupy.

Aging isn't bad, it's just different. It isn't unfair or inappropriate. As the old joke goes, "consider the alternative." But it is a new and more difficult challenge than any we've ever faced—one that caps the others that we've met and surmounted in earlier life.

Robert Browning, the greatest of the Victorian poets, was only 52 but already grappling with the challenges of aging, when he wrote "Rabbi Ben Ezra," his meditation on the beauty of later years. In the first stanza, Browning has Rabbi Ben Ezra say:

"Grow old along with me
The best is yet to be
The last of life for which the first is made..."

Other poets have considered the difficulties and rewards of aging. But I don't think any major modern poet has had the psychological insight of TS Eliot. Eliot shows, in his poem "Little Gidding," a path by which we can age into the peace of self-knowledge: a path that requires us to remain open and curious and non-judgmental about the world. Towards the end of the poem Eliot concludes:

> We shall not cease from exploration
> And the end of all our exploring
> Will be to arrive where we started
> And to know the place for the first time.

How do we do this? How do we remain fresh and open to change? How do we keep on living instead of slowly slipping into mere existing? How do we avoid spending our later years with a mind filled with emptiness and our hand filled with nothing but the TV remote? How do we challenge ourselves to follow the path of acceptance instead of the path of judgment? How do we arrive, finally, at the later years of our lives and know ourselves and those around us for the first time?

It isn't easy. But there's a resource available for us; one we seldom recognize is there. A resource that is in one sense free but that, as Eliot said, "costs not less than everything" because it requires us to examine ourselves through the eyes of others.

That resource is constructive criticism: something we can most easily bear from those we trust—from family and from friends— but that is just as valuable from those we don't like or don't care about.

As for the other parts of our lives, we get feedback every day, whether we want it or not. Sometimes we ignore it, sometimes we resent it, sometimes we discount it and sometimes we don't even realize it's there. If we choose to notice it, to think about it, to accept it, we keep on the path of meeting the responsibilities of our age. We can hope that, as St. Luke said, we "grow in wisdom and age and grace before God and man".

Recently, a dear friend offered some advice that was hard for me to accept. After mulling it over, I realized it was good advice, and that giving it had taken my friend's willingness to put our friendship at risk. No surprise to most of you, my response was to write a poem. Here it is.

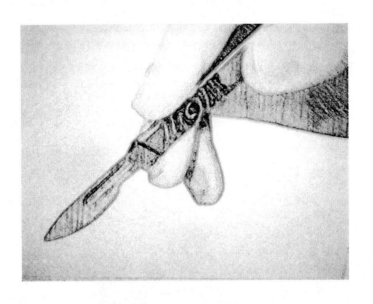

Love's Scalpel

The skillful surgeon wields the steel
Excising the imperfect part
The wound, so sharp but quick to heal
(incisive, brutal healing art)
Repairs, by way of injury
The inner flaw we cannot see.

Kind wisdom is a surgeon's blade
A knife that cuts away the veils
That hide our eyes from games we've played
To bolster our self-serving tales;
Restores the sight obscured within
And rights us on our path again.

Only the shallow know themselves
The heart holds hollows we can't see
A wise friend's insight often give us
Wisdom's sharp revealing key
And how we choose to see this deed
Will make us either heal or bleed.

All wisdom comes from suffering
A clean cut heals with little trace
Your steely wisdom is the thing
That helps me to a state of grace.

November

Autumn's harsh trumpet
White wings under silver skies
Swan slips through thin clouds.

Ducks

November morning
wings cupped and feet extended
Hidden hunter waits

Autumn's swift harvest
tumbles stunned from leaden sky
reaper's booming call

Hawks

Dangerous to the slow and foolish
Living instruments of death
Spillers of blood

And yet they love
Live on the fractured boundary
Between partnership
And solitude

Nest together, fly alone
Hunt together, kill alone

Dog Mountain Haiku

Here's a cosmic truth:
We are all hairs on the back
Of the same black dog.

Nature Red in Tooth and Claw

Six thirty. Sunday morning. Late January
River mist shrouds the cliffs
Dark yields slowly to light as I climb
to a ridge at the treeline

Trees give way to brush and rock
Sudden slapping, staccato squawking
I face the sound
Fear and wildness labor in the branches

White blur. Tattered flailing, ragged clapping
Pale shape jerks jaggedly right into low trees
A barred gray killer, fleet, brutally compact
follows, a beat behind

Heedless, desperate, the snow goose
Wedges into the crotch of a bush below
Hangs shivering, silent. On a branch above
Owl waits.

I climb down the hillside. Owl retreats
eyes me coldly from a post
several trees away
I grasp the gasping goose
lift, toss, and hope. It can't fly far
huddles under low branches downhill

Owl watches

Homecoming

He dreams,
Makes a list of her graces
Her kind, calm heart
Welcoming body, gentle perceptive hands
The thousand other things that
Taken separately
Can be added up
But will not be the whole of her

At the end it's just this
A quiet, half-amused smile
Eyes and mouth equal partners
That welcomes him
And he knows he's home

No Assurance

"Now faith is the assurance of things hoped for,
the conviction of things not seen"

Belief has slipped away
With the years
In the contentious conversation
Between fact and faith
Fact won out

This is sometimes the case
When your maybe
Is rubbed raw
On the rocks of what is.

Somewhere along the way
My karma ran over my dogma
And faith, damaged and bleeding
Had to be put down.

Odysseus: The Harvest of Our Years

We all seek significance in our lives. As children, we want to win games and be popular. As we get older, we collect various forms of power. And we glory in our accomplishments and the accolades they bring us.

But, what of old age? What real significance can our life have

in a society that is so oblivious to the special gifts that we can only offer when we have lived and suffered for the better part of a lifetime?

Browning said "...grow old along with me, the best is yet to be; the last of life for which the first was made...." What possible meaning can this have for a person over 60, living in this wired world?

I believe our greatest significance as we age comes from the example that only we can set; from the clarity we can bring to the world by renouncing the things that no longer matter; by living a life in which we reflect back to the world the wisdom we've paid so great a price to acquire.

The story of the Odyssey illustrates this belief. Like the Iliad, the Odyssey ends in the middle of things. Odysseus has come home. The shrewd strategist has killed the suitors who were besieging his wife Penelope. He is reunited with her, and with his father and his son.

That's where the story ends. It's not an ending that would pass the test of Aristotle' Poetics. Lots of unanswered questions.

But there are actually two endings to Odysseus' story, although only one of them is told by Homer. The other was first told by Dante, and later Tennyson added his meditation on Dante's version.

I'd like to look first at how Dante saw things unfold. In Paradise Lost, Dante portrays Odysseus as unrepentant and unconscious of himself. He suggests that in later years Odysseus, bored and eager for adventure, returns to sea with his crew of men. They sail to the baths of the Western stars and, as they are trying to reach a mountainous island, are swept into a whirlpool and drowned.

For this; for leading his men to death yet again because of his pride and recklessness, Dante too placed Odysseus in the innermost circle of Hades, amongst the "Deceivers."

Homer's epilogue, on the other hand, is easily missed because it takes place in the middle of the poem, when Odysseus is entering Hades to see the dead heroes who fell at Troy. Tiresias, the blind seer, meets him. He prophesies that, after Odysseus returns home, he will set out once again, this time so far into the interior of Ithaca that people there have never seen the sea, or tasted salt.

With him he is to carry a "well cut" oar. He is to plant the oar in the path when he encounters a stranger who asks him about the "winnowing fan" he is carrying. Then, he is to make sacrifice to, Poseidon, the god of the sea: a ram, a bull and a boar. After that, he is to return home and sacrifice to the rest of the gods.

And Tiresias promises him that having done this, he will live to a rich old age, and "...Death will come to you out of the sea, Death in his gentlest guise...."

What is this all about? An oar being called a winnowing fan? Animals being sacrificed to Poseidon?

Lets take the winnowing fan first. A winnowing fan is a broad, oar-like blade that was used by the Greeks to separate the chaff from harvested grain. On a windy day, the grain was tossed into the air with the winnowing fan. The wind would blow the chaff

141

away while the grain fell to the ground.

For Odysseus, the oar had been the primary tool of his adventuring spirit. As an instrument of his skill and courage, the oar separated him from other men. It had taken him places that only he was shrewd and courageous enough to go, and took him back out again, away from danger and off to the next adventure.

So what does it mean for him to plant his oar? By planting his oar, Odysseus is giving up the very thing that is symbolic of how he earned his success and significance in the world.

What about Poseidon? Earlier in the Odyssey, Odysseus and his men landed on the island where Polyphemus, the Cyclops, lived with his sheep. Polyphemus was the son of Poseidon. Not only did Odysseus and his men slaughter and roast some of the sheep, but after they were captured by Polyphemus, they escaped by blinding him. To make things worse, Odysseus taunted Polyphemus about his blindness as they sailed away.

Poseidon's anger at this offense to his son kept Odysseus wandering, unable to reach his home, for ten years.

So, in his old age, Odysseus has two profound items of unfinished business. First, he has to make peace with Poseidon. Equally important, he must give up his old ways of finding significance in the world. He must bring into the world a new significance; one that is grounded in the joys, accomplishments and sufferings of his life.

The Odyssey ends without resolving these questions. But we're free to imagine how things might have turned out. Here's one version, for which I owe a debt of gratitude to the author Helen Luke.

After his return, Odysseus enjoys his reunion with Penelope. He watches the young manhood of his son and the serene age of his father. But he begins thinking about a final voyage on the wine dark sea; a last adventure in a well-built ship with friends and a trusty crew.

One day he sits on a cliff, watching the sea and planning his voyage. It is hot, and he drowses under a tree. In a dream, Tiresias comes and chides him for his blindness.

"Your shrewd mind is a gift from the gods. Too often you have mis-used it, and brought suffering on yourself and others. Here you stand, on the threshold of old age. But the exploits you are planning come from your youthful inner blindness and not from the wisdom that is truly yours."

The dream ends, but Odysseus remains on the cliff watching the sun set. He is ashamed of his failure to see the destructive results of his arrogance: dead companions and the hatred of Poseidon.

Odysseus goes home to Penelope and tells her he will be leaving in the morning. But his path is inland, and his only companions will be his knife and a well cut oar.

In the morning he sets out. After a hard journey, he comes to a crossroads. A stranger watches him approach, and he hears the words that Tiresias spoke so long ago: "What winnowing fan is that on your shoulder?"

Odysseus looks at him, and the stranger continues: "your travels, your achievements and failures, the gains and losses to which your winged ship carried you: all of these were slowly forging for you a winnowing fan. It is the autumn of your life, and now the harvest is in.

Your oar is no longer the force that carries you to new adventures. Rather, it is a symbol of discriminating wisdom, so you can know both the wheat and the chaff in your life; so you can attend to what is truly important."

"And why," asks Odysseus, "should I plant this well cut oar here instead of taking it home? If not for my own use, then for my son?"

The stranger replies, "To leave it is essential. If you put it in your son's hands, you will watch his sea journey through life, and transfer to him your yearning for great deeds. You will never be able to let go of the goals of your youth."

In silence, they dig a hole and place the oar in it, blade up. Then the stranger says he will go to the village to get a ram and a bull for the sacrifice. Odysseus, he says, must go into the wilds to find a boar.

Apprehensively, Odysseus goes into the wilds with only his knife and a rope with a noose. And now he realizes what this sacrifice means: three offerings of the driving power of his masculinity; the power which has carried him through so much, but has cost him so dearly.

He hears a rustling in the undergrowth and steps to the side of the trail. Softly, he calls to the boar that emerges from the trees and approaches him. As if in a trance, he slips the noose over the boar's head, turns and walks slowly down the trail. The boar follows him, the rope dangling loosely. Odysseus is filled with joy, thinking "he comes consenting."

Odysseus and his companion (the god Hermes) build three fires, and shed the blood of sacrifice, offering it to Poseidon. By relinquishing his oar, Odysseus has sacrificed his former self in exchange for the significance that can only come from the wisdom and grace of old age. And by sacrificing the three animals, he has atoned to Poseidon for his treatment of Polyphemus. His enmity with Poseidon is over.

Odysseus goes home, and he grows into a rich old age, weighted with years but light as a breath of wind. And Death comes gently for him out of the sea.

Reward and Punishment

Two brothers, aged single digits
On a raw hillside, red dirt
Scattered with the afterbirth
Of uninspired cold war housing

Nothing else but the wind
And a home-made box kite
Covered with blue tissue
From a Christmas box of apples

The late winter wind is green
With sharp little teeth
That bite through plaid jackets
And muddy jeans

They'll pay for it later
For the mud that covers them
But now there's only the kite
The wind, and the glorious absence
Of adult supervision

A lifetime later
The punishment is forgotten
But the wind, the hill and the kite
Still live.

On the Nature of God's Love

Why does morning's sun strike first
the tree that's broken
by December's storm?

Devolution

Grandmother cared for my mother
and for my mother's cousins, who were orphaned
and my mother took care of me.
A nanny took care of my children
whose children now have, not children
But dogs.
And doggy day care takes care of them.

Each generation has invested less
in that which follows. It makes sense
I guess.

Our attachment's usually not the same
for dogs as it is for children.
With dogs there's seldom suffering
no struggle to love in spite of your brokenness
and that of the broken thing you struggle to love.

We're not stuck for a lifetime
with that first dog; there will be others.
Some more benefits—
no college tuition, no screaming matches,
no unanswered calls, no forgotten birthdays.
So, why take the risk?

Wonder where this is going?
If we love our pets enough
will they eventually become the perfect children
we never, really, could have had?

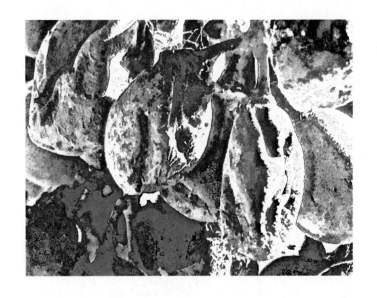

Ode to Sauterne

Sing in praise of shriveled grapes
Praise their desiccated sweetness
Bless the length of time it takes
To reach their overripe completeness

Scorn the fresh, the just-picked fruit
Mourn its immaturity
For age brings texture, depth and truth
While youth has merely purity

Sunday Inventory

Fresh damp coolness in the air
Geese calling from the lake: feathered clarinets
The river's fast muddy thickness
A half-remembered canyon trail

Young buds: red and green, urgent
The summit in thin fog
Red berries along the slippery trail
A haiku arrives

A bench on the trail in sharp green wind
New daffodils—Persephone returned
Cold hands as he taps the keys
Her warm spirit, always somewhere near

On the Downslope

What matters the most
In these years on the downslope:
Our children and friends

Appointment in Samarra

Got to get out of here.
This relationship is killing me.
Or maybe it's the town or this job, or the weather
or the too-familiar story
I seem to cycle through.
Whatever.

Nothing changes.
Everything in the rear view mirror
is catching up again.
Past and future smeared together
A never-ending present that always brings me
circling back to where I started.

No more re-runs;
I need to switch to a new channel
Need to trade in
the old familiar ending
for a new happily ever after
a new love, a new look, a new town,
a new last chance to get it right
for once and for all.

Stay or go. That's the eternal question.
And our answer always finds us.

Christmas

This is not about Christmas.

Well, sort of. It isn't an exhortation to be good for Santa, or to remember the birth of Christ. We've all had our full supply of that over the years, and this year is not going to be an exception.

What interests me is that all cultures and religions in temperate climates around the world have some sort of major celebration around the time of the New Year. And I started asking myself why that would be, and what meaning it has in my busy life.

The year winds down. In temperate climates, the sun comes to work later and goes home a little earlier every day. The grass turns brown and plants die. The harvest is in. And even those of us who live in the city can feel the pace of things shift. Late fall brings red leaves and a cold white sunlight that I've never particularly cared for. Mixed in with the beauty of the changing leaves is the scent of death.

Not to jolly, huh? And yet, how necessary. The dying of the year leads, always, to the peace of winter and the rebirth of Spring.

At least, we in our comfort and knowledge can say we know that. But you don't have to turn the clock back very far to find a time when no one took the return of Spring for granted.

Thinking of all this a few years ago, I stepped out on my terrace for a look at my awakening garden. The intense green of the daffodils as they pushed up through the damp dirt reminded me of the Greek myth of Persephone, who became wife to the subterranean god Hades but who was allowed to return to the upper world each year, bringing spring and new life with her.

Persephone

That girl is back; she
ran away from her husband again.
It's an annual occurrence.

I found her in my garden this morning:
tight green dress and cloud-gray eyes.

She won't stay, but
we'll love each other
for a while.

New Year Resolutions

The old year is in the rear view mirror. Once again, we stumble hopefully into the New Year.

I used to think all the talk of New Year's resolutions was just some sort of cultural artifact; maybe the result of our country's rich and variegated religious, racial and cultural stew. Look closer, though. You find that all places in which there are seasons also have had, for ages, some sort of ceremony for saying "my bad" for the acts of the past year, and "I'll do better next time" for the coming year.

This impulse is ancient; well beyond recorded history. No doubt if you're huddled in an unheated mud hut for the winter, with three unbathed generations crowded together with the fragrant dogs for warmth and subsisting on a diet of last year's wild garlic, you have a lot of time to think about how things could be better the next time around.

Yet there's something fresh and clean about the winter. Hopeful, even. When New Year's comes, we know we've moved through the worst of the dark. We can sense a new start as the days lengthen and the midnight blues of dawn and dusk are more evenly spaced each day. We know that, once again, we've been given a new beginning.

I think mankind has always felt a deep gratitude for that new beginning; for the knowledge that we get another chance to nudge our lives a little more into the center of the path. By writing down our resolutions, we acknowledge to ourselves (and those to whom we show them) our failures of the past. We also make a public announcement of our determination that this New Year will be a new and improved model. Nothing puts the pressure on like a public announcement.

I've got my own resolutions this year, and they have a lot to do with living the best life I can in the remaining time I've got. I have spent far too much time worrying about what isn't, instead of being grateful for what is. There's some good raw material there for a few stiff resolutions.

I won't tell my resolutions to you, but I will write them down and work hard on keeping them. In the meantime, here's something I wrote. I hope you'll enjoy it while you're writing down your own.

Now, stop chewing on that garlic, kick the dogs out, and get to work on those resolutions.

Unreliable Narrator

What do you see?
Not much. It's foggy out.

But, what do you see?
Gray sky and fog. Maybe some trees
And the corner of a building
Across the street

But, what do you see?
A pale gray veil
Over poplars in the park
Sad faint yellow light
On buildings wrapped in tissue
That dissolve pallidly to nothing

Winter morning.

January Sunrise

New Winter morning
In the warm afterwards, we
Laugh at the pale sun

Golden Haired Lion

Another year
More companions sick or dead, as
The current speeds up

My long river of choice and chance
Nears the sea
Where all beginnings and ends converge
At eternity's gate
And night and day expire

Love, once given
Can be repented, can be recalled
But cannot be reclaimed
No regrets

I am a golden haired lion
I watch the dying sun
And remember
The furnace whispers for me
But I will not burn

The only true sin
Is forgetting

For Lucretius

The gods are finally dead
Departed under an empty sky darker than evening
Nothing of the sun remains
but bruised clouds
and bitter cobalt rain

All things go to the grave
And so with each of us
Worn out by the long years
Borne by the weeping
That walks only with death

But life persists
Morning arrives with its bright lances
Pours out the new day
from Apollo's bowl
and the funeral chant is mingled
with the cries of newborns
coming to this world of light.

Fog

Thin December fog
Caught soft in naked branches
Lemon winter sun.

Resurrection

Morning arrives: an insistent beggar
Clutching the chilly clothes
It shuffled off in yesterday
Lemon light floods under ice blue sky
We wake again, hoping salvation
Arrived in the night.

We're each the center of our universe,
The world refracted through
The imperfect lens of ourselves
Each night is a little death
Each morning we are born again.

Asleep we dream of morning
Dream we'll rise, beautiful and new.

Spring Again

Spring arrives; with it,
A seasonal disregard
For the worst-case scenario
As days unwind and the blessings
Always outweigh my burdens.

Astarte's crescent arcs across
The April night.
Cherry trees shiver, shake themselves;
Petals floating past on Easter air.

Surviving winter pansies
Glare at the world
From their altar on my terrace.

It's a new world again;
Right here, right now, every second
Flooded with God's green beauty.
There's just no time to worry
About tomorrow.

A Sense of the City

Smell

In the foreground, the smooth harshness of my cigar, a black Partagas Maduro, almost overpowers the other smells of the evening. Milder, but still with its own hot edge, the bouquet of the cognac in my glass floats in the air. It's Sunday evening, and the weekday industrial smell of the foundry a few miles distant has been swept away. The wind that blows over the west hills from the coast brings the smell of spring, of growing things resurrected from their winter burial, the faint evening smell of the firs in Forest Park, and a growing hint—warm wetness and sea water—that rides on the west wind and promises rain tomorrow.

Underneath it all, there's the indefinable smell that says "city." It's not just the rude ancient smell of burning coal that still sometimes hangs in the Portland air each winter, long after the last coal fired furnace has been converted to oil. It's more a mysterious aggregation; the odors of the ten thousand things that, only in the city, take place unremarked and yet shape our deep conviction of what a place smells like. As the light leaves the sky, the smells of the day dissolve. They'll return in the morning.

Light

Late afternoon in February. Looking west, there's a new 30-story condo construction next door. The sky is filled with roiling light gray clouds, pierced through with a shadow of sunlight along the east/west axis; an inverted canyon with light at its bottom, just out of sight. You can infer blue sky in some of the crevices between the clouds.

As the light fades, a small jet flies north along the ridge, on approach to PDX. It's mid winter; half way to spring. Suddenly, there's more and better light at 5:00 in the evening than we've had since early November. Somehow, I think we're deeply linked to all this; not just passive observers but active participants in the journey towards summer. Let's walk together towards all those tomorrows.

Sound

From my terrace, the distant growl of trucks on the freeway and the white noise hiss of their tires—distant surf rolling in from a storm far out at sea. A small twin engined plane follows the well beaten path along the top of the west hills to land at PDX. If I listen carefully, I can just barely hear the low buzzing of its turbos. A cool breeze circles around the terrace, which is in a partly sheltered nook of my building.

The air is silent, except for the faint rustle of the bamboo leaves along my wall and the invisible noise the faint wind makes in the bare branches of the trees below; more of a feeling, a sense of presence, than a sound. The birches rise up from five stories below and wave their bare branches at me. Coolness creeps into my fingers. Down on Tenth Avenue, a Harley rumbles slowly by, oblivious to the heavens, and rides up the street under the timeless return of Venus and a thin crescent moon. A street car's muffled clanking and electrical whine fade up Northrup. Another day.

Light and Sound

Soft gray cloud cover and soft gray "end of the week" light echo off the streets and buildings. A luminous gray mist, the color of the tired week, wraps the street. The west hills are invisible but still, somehow, present. A train labors in the distance, gently muffled by the gray light. Its whistle has the sound of a lonesome metal creature calling to its mate. I fix my dinner and reflect on my blessings.

Gray

An Alaska Airlines jet makes the long downwind leg over the west hills on its way to PDX. People coming home after a long week and visitors coming in for the weekend. Behind it the sky is a high solid dome of pearl. Lower down are cumulus clouds in 50 shades of gray. The sun is setting somewhere out there but, perhaps out of modesty, hides its naked splendor behind the clouds. Even the light is gray. Everything feels muted and tired. For those I love and for myself, I pray for peace and renewal this weekend.

Descent into Night

The construction guys on the condo across the way got a lot done today, and the pounding and clanging have almost stopped. The sky is that strange blue white color that's bright and yet carries within it the shade of evening. As the sun sinks behind the west hills, the light grows cold. With the sun out of sight, it's clear this is was a sunny day in January, and not a sunny day in April.

The west hills are almost black, but the trees still have an almost indiscernible hint of dark green. Directly above, the sky shades seamlessly from pale lemon yellow through yellow-tinged pink to pale blue and finally, overhead, the crepuscular blue that is almost black. Shot through the pale blue is a note of midnight, though you can't really see it; you just feel it on the periphery of your vision as you stare at the late evening sky. Venus is about 20 degrees above the hills and burns with that brightness the Greeks interpreted as passion.

Council Crest

On the top. Strong east winds and high cirrus clouds. The air is cold crystal, with just a trace of haze. It's sunny and the wind has the woodsy earthy smell of early spring. Below, Portland hides under a tight cap of fog. It's getting cold—time to head back down the hill. The warmth of the car is not as compelling as the view from the ridge I'm sitting on, but it draws me nonetheless. I can always return.

Spring Walk

31 varieties of blooming plants so far today. Spring is here! New growth, a new beginning, resurrection from the old and the cold. A new chance for the beauty of right action to infuse our lives. Without that, the flowers have little meaning

Sunday, above the Zoo

Sitting on my bench above the zoo at the outermost end of the Maple Trail. The cool wind carries a riot of early flower smells as it hurries indifferently past me on its Spring business. The insistent white noise hiss of the Sunset Highway below is backdrop for the softer, more immediate sound of the wind through the new leaves and grass on the hillside. What was, in winter, a far view of the hills is newly blocked by the first foliage on the rare maples that surround my bench.

As I walk home in the moist Sunday morning air, I think how grateful I am for my life. It's the only one I've got, but it's pretty wonderful. Now, all I need is that winning lottery ticket.

Borrowed Words

I have to admit my own poetry has been made up by choosing, from the entire store of words which the best poets have used, their very best words; those charged with ambiguity, color, and with complex and shifting meaning.

Everywhere here are borrowed phrases and ideas. And they have not picked out by untidy footnotes or quotation marks. I offer the words in these poems as my exclusive possessions.

In my view, the great lords of poetry are pleased to see the occasional tradesman setting up his booth under their castle walls, and dealing in their proven products.

At least, were I one of them, I would certainly be happy if anyone found a phrase of mine worth lifting.

TE Lawrence—*Seven Pillars of Wisdom*

The Photographs of Jim Halliday

These photos by Jim Halliday are presented by the invitation of and in collaboration with the author, not as strict illustration, but as complementary art.

Pages: 16, 20, 27, 32, 34, 40, 42, 48, 54, 55, 56, 58, 60, 64, 68, 70, 103, 107, 112, 114, 120, 130, 132, 140, 144, 146, 150, 160, 162, & 164.

Colophon

The text of this book is set in Garamond Premier Pro, designed for Adobe by Robert Slibach between 2005–2007 as a reinterpretation of the designs of Claude Garamond's metal punches and type designs of the mid-1500s, as well as on the italic designs of Garamond's contemporary, Robert Granjon. Titles are set in Ocean Sans, designed for Monotype in 1997 by Ong Chong Wah.

CPSIA information can be obtained
at www.ICGtesting.com
Printed in the USA
FSOW01n1651260517
34473FS